AUTHOR

Destery Hildenbrand

Destery Hildenbrand is an extended reality solution architect with Intellezy. He has more than 17 years of experience in training and development and seven years focusing on immersive technologies. His primary focus is helping organizations plan, design, and develop engaging learning experiences through immersive technology.

Content Manager, Technology Application
Alexandria Clapp

Editor, *TD at Work*
Patty Gaul

Managing Editor
Joy Metcalf

Senior Graphic Designer
Shirley E.M. Raybuck

Training teams are always looking for ways to engage learners and improve delivery and information retention. They do so in a variety of ways, such as online learning modules, virtual classrooms, instructor-led sessions, and multimedia. However, direct practice or live-action walkthroughs can be missing in training programs. Those are vital because they enable learners to connect the information with action.

Consider the 70-20-10 model, which is based on the principle that 10 percent of the learning process happens in the classroom, 20 percent happens informally, and 70 percent is experiential and comes from practicing the skills. That 70 percent could be via a step-by-step procedural process or a crucial conversation with a leader or co-worker.

Although ideal, the 70-20-10 model is not always practical. What if the skills are dangerous, such as operating an open pit mine or oil rig? What if they are expensive to re-create because they involve costly equipment or you can't replicate locations and procedures?

Because of the potential hazards learners may face, sometimes as L&D professionals, we cannot send learners into the field to start practicing. Yet, we need to equip them with the necessary skills to do their job well. That's where virtual reality comes in.

This technology stands out for experiential training because it doesn't compromise learners' safety and provides the direct practice learners need. VR is versatile—we can re-create dangerous or harsh conditions for practicing such skills as operating complex, heavy machinery as well as office settings or shopping centers for customer service skills practice.

In this issue of *TD at Work*, I will:

- Review the different versions of extended reality.
- Detail the skills and team members necessary for creating VR programs.
- Explain the process for developing VR content.
- Explore case studies for using VR for learning.

Reality Check

While VR has been around since the 1960s, it has only recently found itself in a more prominent consumer position, thanks to improvements in the hardware and software market. According to data that analytics company ARtillery Intelligence collected, the demand for VR is projected to grow to more than 12 billion by 2024. ARtillery also points out that an estimated 23 percent of households now own or use a VR headset.

Before I delve into the ways you can use this technology for L&D, let's review the foundational knowledge of what VR—or, more accurately, CGI VR—is and how it fits into the immersive technology landscape, which is often referred to as extended reality. XR is the umbrella term that groups VR, augmented reality, mixed reality, and 360-degree video. It's helpful to know the similarities and differences between those technologies because they each can provide solutions for different types of learning problems.

CGI Virtual Reality

With CGI VR, a person is completely immersed in a VR world via a headset. They are transported to another time or place with the ability to explore and interact. CGI VR experiences can simulate working on an oil rig, take users into an open pit mine, put them on a busy street performing at an on-site utility location, or enable them to have an office conversation with an artificial employee. The possibilities, places, and interactions are customizable to your organization's learning needs.

An essential distinction of CGI VR from other immersive options is that it is an entirely computer-generated virtual space. VR experiences rely on high-end graphics and visuals to be as true to life as possible when re-creating scenes. Even with that ability, they are still distinguishable from a live environment. Developers and 3D artists create VR environments with the authoring and design tools often used in video game design.

Use cases: Consider these cases when you may want to use CGI VR as part of your learning portfolio:

- The process, procedure, or skill is dangerous to practice in the real world.
- The cost of traveling or using tools in training is high. CGI VR provides reusable, high-dollar process training for a fixed cost. Think in terms of refilling or replacing extinguishers after training or taking a tool or machine off of the production line.

Figure 1.
Extended Reality Technologies

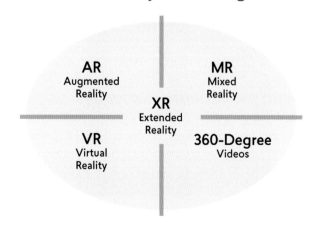

- Training requires exceptionally specialized environments, such as simulating a walk on Mars, diving with a submarine, working on an oil rig for repairs, or refueling an aircraft in-flight.
- The task is repetitive and requires consistent, repeatable actions before the learner executes the steps correctly. Those may be soft skill conversations, properly assembling a widget, or landing a plane.

I can't emphasize enough that when considering CGI VR as a learning solution, this learning modality is most beneficial when used to fit into one of these or similar use cases. CGI VR experience works best not as a stand-alone application but as part of a blended learning solution as a way to practice skills or as a means of active learning reinforcement.

Augmented Reality

AR is the digital overlay of information onto the real world. AR can include any type of media you would put into an e-learning module. The technology keeps users in the real world. Most AR experiences are built for mobile devices because those devices are readily available, contain consumers' necessary components, and align with users' capabilities and adoption. According to consumer data company Statista, in 2021, there were 800 million mobile AR users versus 410,000 AR headset users globally.

AR experiences are most effective when providing needed information at a specific time or location. For example, if a user needs help transitioning from one step to the next in a process, AR can provide guidance and identify a safe pathway for doing so.

Use cases: Use AR as a performance support tool or as a means of accessing guidance from others when in a remote location. For example, workers can scan a code to find step-by-step instructions. Or they can use AR glasses or other smart technology for remote guidance, such as to troubleshoot a problem.

Mixed Reality

Mixed reality has the same capabilities as AR but enhances the digital overlay experience by recognizing and interacting with the world around the user. Mixed reality is an evolution of AR that relies on environmental recognition—such as walls, floors, or other objects in the room—to enable digital content to appear more naturally in the space.

Use cases: MR experiences can bring a user's environment to life with new furniture or seeing whether a new TV will fit on the wall or enabling a person to try on an outfit with a specific pair of shoes. As a learning tool, MR provides a more interactive, deeply engaging experience.

360-Degree Video

Also called VR or sometimes *immersive video* (more on that next), 360-degree videos—sometimes shortened to 360 *video* or even 360—are recorded with a specialty camera and then stitched together into a sphere. They include all

---

CGI Virtual Reality Use Cases

While I don't recommend using CGI VR as a stand-alone application in any field, there are many industries where this type of training can be beneficial as part of a learning package. For example, these industries are using immersive reality:

- Construction for project and assembly visualization
- Automotive for vehicle repair and virtual dealership tours
- Aviation for repair work and training for hard-to-see components
- Field service for remote assistance and guidance
- Military and defense for military training, such as communicating and managing stress in combat situations and real-time recognition
- Insurance for claim handling and inspection simulation
- Healthcare for working with patients with dementia and for surgery practice
- Corporate for leadership training and soft skills development

Those use cases and industry examples are just some of what's happening with CGI VR today. The list is not meant to limit what is possible nor exclude any industry or use case. Rather, it is intended as a stepping stone when thinking of how CGI VR can be a valuable addition to your L&D portfolio and keep building from there.

sides and angles of the recorded area, putting the user in the middle of the video or image with content all around them. 360 videos can be immersive when the user wears a VR headset, or users can watch the videos via a mobile device or webpage.

Use cases: 360 video is an excellent option for virtual tours, immersive storytelling, and high-level hot spot interactive engagements.

CGI VR vs. 360-Degree Video

Of all the XR terms, VR is used most inconsistently. Most uses of VR tend to encompass anything consumed through a wearable headset. That leads to grouping CGI VR and 360 videos in the same definition. While they seem similar from a high-level view, it's essential to recognize the fundamental differences between them so you are better prepared and informed when planning your next immersive technology project.

CGI VR is fundamentally different from 360 videos. As mentioned, it is a computer-generated, fully immersive, interactable 3D re-creation of an environment and its objects. It is entirely adaptable to users' needs. 360 videos are immersive, spherical video recordings captured by an omnidirectional camera. The fidelity is high because it is a video of a more realistic environment. However, the experience is limited to that medium. Traditional editing methods provide the length, image, and story you want to convey. With authoring tools, you can add interactive hot spots or additional text and imagery in the scene, but it will always remain a static video.

Users actively participate in the CGI VR experience. Their vantage point is within their control. They can change their viewing angle and location by using a controller. They can pick up, throw, break, repair, or move objects inside the experience and take part in anything happening in the scene.

With a 360 video, user interactivity is minimal. Users cannot physically move around within the video and cannot directly interact with any objects. They cannot pick up, push, pull, or move levers. 360 video enables users to observe the actions happening in the video. The camera placement and capture dictate their role in the story, whether in the action or in the crowd.

Both CGI VR and 360 videos have their place and can enable successful learning depending on your project's needs. To put a final point on the differences, each has a unique development cycle and production efforts. A CGI project will require 3D artists and developers to work together to create the immersive environment; a 360-video project will run like a video shoot with post-production efforts. Likewise, each has different development paths and costs. Keeping those differences in mind is essential to ensure the success of your L&D project and learners' or clients' satisfaction with the outcome.

CGI VR for Learning

To get started with creating VR training programs, you and your team will need specific skills and the right people to bring the programs to fruition.

A typical learning team has 80 percent of the skills necessary to prepare, design, and deliver a VR experience. Those include problem solving; project managing; and planning, designing, building, and deploying learning experiences via various modalities. The remaining 20 percent required to bring the experience to life are additional skills not typically learned in most L&D roles.

- **3D modeling:** creating, animating, assembling, and streamlining environments and assets for use in VR
- **Unity/Unreal development:** assembling the 3D environment and assets into the scene, programming the scenario, and building the end package for deployment
- **Device management:** scaling and deploying the experience to headsets and managing the content
- **Experience API data management:** capturing and ingesting Experience API data into a learning record store and funneling that data into SCORM-ready packages

To create VR programs, you will need the following team members. If your organization has the individuals with these skills, you could fill the roles internally, or you can partner with a vendor.

- **Project manager** keeps the project on track, on time, and on budget.
- **Instructional designer** ensures the learning problem is articulated, drives the experience from start to

finish, and ensures the experience is storyboarded and planned in a way that maximizes the VR delivery medium; depending on the project, you may have more than one instructional designer.

- **Content creator** creates videos, images, branding guidelines, user interface/user experience layouts,

---

Virtual Reality Terms to Know

Tethered: This is a VR headset that attaches to a computer to function.

Untethered: This is a VR headset that does not require a computer connection.

Three degrees of freedom (3DoF): This indicates that users can move their head up and down, pivot left and right, and look left and right.

Six degrees of freedom (6DoF): This means users can do the same movements as 3DoF and walk around.

Mobile device management: Third-party apps and websites manage mobile device content, including VR headsets.

Haptics: This is feedback in the form of resistance, a buzz, or vibration to indicate an interaction.

Eye tracking: Sensors in the headset track the user's eye position rather than their head movement.

Head tracking: Sensors track the user's head position. The user can look up, down, left, and right.

Field of view: This is the measurement of the visual field inside the headset.

Frame rate: Measured in frames per second, this indicates the number of images shown in a second. Video is typically played back at 30 fps for steady viewing, while VR should run at a minimum of 72 fps to avoid disorientation and motion sickness.

---

or illustrations; again, depending on the project, you may have more than one.

- **Visual designer** helps craft the overall style or brand of the experience and works closely with the instructional designer and client to ensure the experience achieves the right aesthetic.
- **UI/UX designer** assists in planning how users will interact with the VR experience and researches how it's being done now and what will or won't work within the current plan; this role is recommended but not required.
- **3D modeler** creates models from scratch to represent the necessary environments, objects, and avatars; the individual's tasks may include animations and rigging and light work with the software development kit for assembly.
- **Developer (Unity/Unreal)** primarily works within the software tool; connects the software development kit to the assets and environment from the modelers; and authors the scenarios with movement, interaction, and progression. This individual should have a background in either Unity real-time development or Unreal game development engines. Once assembled, the developer will also export the correct package for use on the designated hardware.

The team will vary for each project. In many cases, one person can fill multiple roles. The most important takeaway is that building for VR requires some skills that your team may not have, so you may need to look elsewhere for that expertise.

VR Tools

In addition to the right skills and individuals, you will need to use a variety of tools to develop the VR program. The software and hardware options I discuss next are not exhaustive; new tools are coming to market all the time, and others are going away. Use this as a starting point and then conduct your own research into what you will need.

Software

Unity real-time development engine and Unreal engine. These are the two main software development options. Each tool can use the software development kits needed to build content for the different hardware on the market today.

Codeless authoring tools. These cloud-based tools are new to the CGI VR development space. You can use them to edit VR experiences. They work the same as Captivate or Storyline for e-learning development and require similar skills for editing content. Storyflow by Motive and CoPilot by Talespin are two examples. Storyflow is built by programmers for learning professionals and gives users control over their content. Users can easily create straightforward procedures, branching narratives, or full-blown simulations. CoPilot enables users to create dynamic conversational learning content where learners practice role play with emotionally realistic virtual humans. Both take an existing environment and assets and give users the ability to edit content within the CGI VR environment. Each software option has different strengths and possesses the key behavior for the VR 2.0 workflow (discussed in the next section), enabling learning teams to take control of their content creation and editing in CGI VR without the need to code.

Hardware

Hardware—that is, headset—options for immersive VR experiences can be tethered or untethered. Tethered headsets require a computer to function fully, making for a higher-quality experience. They use the computer's processing and graphics power to run the experience entirely. The quality of the build components for your desktop or laptop in a tethered setup will drive the quality of the VR experience. However, being attached to a computer limits the user's movement and adds additional cost. Among the tethered headsets currently on the market are the HTC Vive Pro 2, HP Reverb G2, and the Valve Index VR Kit.

Untethered or standalone devices provide a true anytime-anywhere experience when not attached to a computer. Untethered devices are usually cheaper, thus more scalable hardware options for companies. The cost of decoupling is a slight drop-off in graphics and processing power. The main players in the untethered space are the Meta Quest, HTC Vive Focus, and Pico Neo headsets.

Regardless of which type, understand the specifications and keep them in mind when selecting a headset.

Resolution. This is measured per eye in VR headsets. The higher the resolution, the sharper, clearer, and more detailed the objects will be. Low resolution can cause visible pixelization and cause eye strain for some users.

Field of view. This is measured in degrees and indicates how much a user can see in front and peripherally when facing forward. The limit to human vision is 220 degrees of peripheral vision. FOV for headsets will vary. A narrower FOV will appear to close off the scene's edges, like having blinders in place. A wider FOV enables users to see as much of the scene as possible when immersed.

Interpupillary distance. This is the distance between pupils. When IPD is off and the lenses are not positioned correctly, the experience can be blurring and cause discomfort. Adjustable IPD is recommended to ensure maximum user flexibility and comfort.

Refresh rate. Ideally, you want a refresh rate of 90 frames per second to ensure comfort and provide the best headset experience possible. A lower refresh rate can cause blurriness, disorientation, and general discomfort to learners.

Development Workflows

Before you start your first project, it's ideal to understand the workflow. Whether your internal team or an outside vendor handles production, you will likely follow the VR 1.0 and VR 2.0 workflows. CGI VR programs can be lengthy and, at times, costlier than other learning modalities. But with the correct use case, CGI VR is an engaging and effective way to deliver training that fits.

VR 1.0
This is the common workflow for developing most L&D VR experiences. The L&D team directs the development but typically is not skilled in the development tools necessary to build the VR experience.

The group authors the scenarios as best it can according to the provided detailed plan. Once the development team completes an iteration of the VR experience, the group sends that to you and your learning team for review. You compile any adjustments or updates and send those to the development team to complete. Repeat that flow until you are satisfied with the VR experience.

The flow starts with you and your team conducting a needs analysis and planning a detailed storyboard. From there, the development team assembles the environment and configures the assets for Unity or Unreal. You and your team then handle the rest of the workflow, content authoring, reviewing, and making changes using a codeless software tool.

Maintaining content control of the VR program within the L&D team eliminates the need for costly development cycles. That also keeps you and your team—the most knowledgeable people—in charge of adjusting content. Remember that regardless of how content is authored, you need to work with a development team to create environments, assets, and configurations.

VR 2.0
The most significant difference between VR 1.0 and 2.0 is that 2.0 allows for the L&D team—not the developers—to create and author scenarios. The flow starts with you and your team conducting a needs analysis and planning a detailed storyboard. From there, the development team assembles the environment and configures the assets for use in Unity or Unreal. You and your team then handle the rest of the workflow, content authoring, reviewing, and making changes using a codeless software tool.

Figure 2. VR 1.0 Workflow

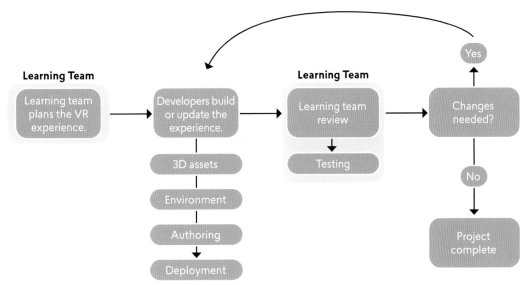

Figure 3. VR 2.0 Workflow

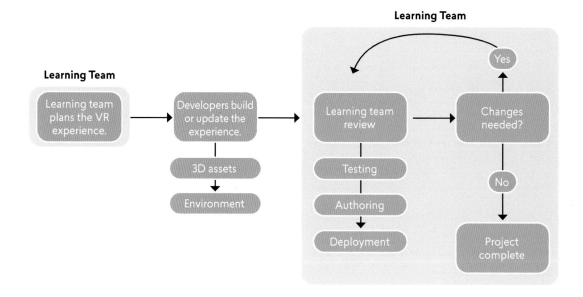

Maintaining content control of the VR program within the L&D team eliminates the need for costly development cycles. It also keeps your team in control of the content, which you know the most about. Keep in mind that regardless of how content is authored, you still need to work with a development team to create environments, assets, and configurations.

Barriers

As with any project, you will encounter barriers that slow or impede your progress. You may have already started identifying some of those potential barriers, including organizational culture issues. Before pitching a CGI VR program to stakeholders, you must fully understand what the technology can and cannot do. You will encounter barriers that slow or impede progress.

Conduct thorough research. Buy a VR headset and some existing experiences, and explore. Look at the latest studies regarding VR and learning, and familiarize yourself with current trends. Statista, ARtillery Intelligence, and PwC have studies that will help you understand the immersive technology landscape and provide significant case study results (see Resources and Additional Reading).

There are many factors involved in securing buy-in for VR programs: costs, return on investment, IT capabilities, team dynamics, skill sets, and feasibility—to name a few. Extensive knowledge and research about the technology and tools needed to build and deploy your L&D initiative will help you reduce barriers. So will identifying a need or problem within the organization that CGI VR will solve.

Go into any potential pitch meeting with as much information as possible. If you can't explain why this is valuable to the company, the conversation will be over almost before it begins. Using technology for the sake of technology is a recipe for disaster. It would be impossible to list all potential barriers. Face them as they arise, and work with your team and organization to solve them as they arise.

Case Studies

While I could call out all the benefits of VR for L&D, that may not be enough to convince you to take a leap and try this technology as a learning solution in your organization. Let's look at three case studies so you can see CGI VR at play in the real world.

Hazard Identification: PASS Training

The US Mine Safety and Health Administration, an agency within the US Department of Labor, works to keep US miners safe from illnesses, injuries, and death while also promoting safe and healthy workplaces for them. The mining process is hazardous, and miners must follow a proper safety protocol to stay free from harm. MSHA plays a vital role in developing and enforcing that protocol.

It had a need for customized content on mining safety that was available in different modalities. To meet that need, MSHA, in partnership with the South Dakota School of Mines, worked with a VR vendor to build a VR full-scale mine environment for new and existing miners to explore and identify potential safety hazards safely and repeatedly. In the discovery process, the team explored the necessary elements to make the environment feel realistic, the hazards to include, what those look like in real life, the goals for learners, and how learners would access the experience. During planning, the team determined that the virtual environment would be an open, working rock quarry. The scene would include a large pit with an excavator actively moving rocks into a processor. To provide realism, the team also determined it would include essential details such as the sound of the excavator and the clang of the falling stones.

The team worked with its VR vendor to deliver a single environment with an opportunity for the user to explore and discover potential hazards to practice mining safety measures and increase awareness in a pit mine. The total experience takes users five to 15 minutes.

This technology stands out for experiential training because it doesn't compromise learners' safety and provides the direct practice learners need.

That short length will save miners time in the future and reduce the risk for the mine, helping MSHA continue in its mission to protect miners.

Early results indicate that material retention improved by 32 percent compared to traditional in-person training. One month after training, retention was at 86 percent, compared to 11 percent from in-person training.

Western University: Personal Support Worker Training

Through a grant from the Future Skills Centre, a federal consortium of public and private partners, Ontario, Canada-based Western University developed a VR training program—Be Epic VR—to help its staff care for people with dementia. Standard personal support worker training addresses skills such as feeding, bathing, and moving patients from their beds or chairs. The list of duties for visits can be long and time-consuming, and nurses can have a tendency to be more focused on the task than the individual.

Patients with dementia have complicated communication impairments. For personal support workers to tend well to their patients' needs, they must go beyond the task-focused skills. The Be Epic VR learning program, which has proved to be successful, was converted from an in-person role play using live actors to a VR immersive experience. The VR program uses characters Nala and James as avatars with middle-stage dementia, and conversational artificial intelligence guides learners in place of live actors. The program developed three separate scenarios for assessment, practice, reflection, and evaluation.

The conversion has led to flexibility in delivery times, locations, and scalability. Further, the format enables personal support workers to practice any time they can and anywhere they have a Wi-Fi signal. This unique medium and approach enables them to practice and fail without consequence.

Ken Blanchard Companies: Building Trust Training

Trust is critical in the workplace and is especially crucial between managers and their direct reports. Trust can increase employee performance and retention, spur creativity and innovation, and expand collaboration. The

> **CGI VR experience works best ... as part of a blended learning solution as a way to practice skills or as a means of active learning reinforcement.**

Ken Blanchard Companies—a global management training, consulting, and coaching company—recently partnered with a VR platform vendor to develop the Building Trust training program, a safe place for supervisors and employees to practice developing and restoring trust.

Learners use a VR online simulation to have realistic conversations about common workplace exchanges with a virtual team member and boost their confidence in trust building. The program has two modules—one to help learners recognize trust issues and another to rebuild trust. Learners can use a VR headset or stream them on their computer.

Conclusion

To start your VR journey, take into consideration the information in this issue as well as via other resources. Take your time, and involve as many stakeholders as possible—especially early on in the process—and get their feedback. Weigh the following factors to begin the conversation with your team and broader organization.

Is VR the right approach? A recent Nielsen global survey found that nearly two-thirds of respondents are routinely turning to technology to help manage and simplify their lives. The same study also uncovered that more than half are willing to look at immersive technology to assist them. VR provides a unique way to experience, engage, and learn through a hands-on approach. But it's only as good as the problem it's solving. Before you pursue VR as a training solution, identify the problem you want to solve, and determine whether VR is the right solution to address it.

VR brings training to life. Finding an effective and engaging way to approach learning challenges is difficult. VR may be the ideal training solution when you can't easily reproduce training situations, the expense to re-create is extensive, or the skill or behavior you're teaching puts learners in danger.

VR offers effective learning opportunities. According to research, learners who have extended reality experiences complete them faster, retain more information, and develop a stronger emotional connection to the content. Studies show that effectiveness and retention in VR rates are higher than in other learning options. When finished, learners' confidence also tracked higher in soft skills, according to a PwC study.

To put that in perspective, think about a recent training course you developed or attended. Imagine how effective it would have been if you could have created an avatar to converse with learners. What would the training experience have looked like if learners could have grabbed things, moved them around, and explored a new environment?

VR presents many possibilities. With a good use case, the right team, and a vision to improve learning opportunities for learners, you can enhance your existing training programs and endeavor to create unforgettable, engaging, and effective future training as well.

I hope that this issue of *TD at Work* has excited you and expanded your confidence in considering VR for L&D. While not every training solution will work in CGI VR, pairing the technology with the proper use case can create a powerful, engaging, and effective learning experience. Good luck on your VR journey.

Books

Knowles, M.S., E.F. Holton III, and R.A. Swanson. 2012. *The Adult Learner*, 7th ed. Abingdon-on-Thames, England: Routledge.

Lombardo, M.M., and R.W. Eichinger. 2000. *The Career Architect Development Planner*, 3rd ed. Minneapolis: Lominger.

Online Resources

Alsop, T. 2022. "Augmented Reality (AR) – Statistics & Facts." Statista, October 22. statista.com/topics/3286/augmented-reality-ar.

ATD Research. 2018. "UPS: Driving Results Through Virtual Reality and Simulation-Based Training." January. td.org/research-reports/ups.

Boland, M. 2021. "New Report: VR Revenue to Reach $12.2 Billion by 2024." ARtillery Intelligence, February 20. thevrara.com/blog2/2019/2/20/will-ars-killer-app-be-social-new-report-rwccm-g8ajl-e4sr5-b9f9r-gt64y-5e3e8-asrs2-d9xry-ymp6b-7s7bl-cbtsm-39bwj.

Bonilla, D.R. 2021. "Future Workplace: The Viability of VR and AR for Business and Learning Professionals." ATD blog, March 18. td.org/atd-blog/future-workplace-the-viability-of-vr-and-ar-for-business-and-learning-professionals.

Likens, S., and A. Mower. 2022. "What Does Virtual Reality and the Metaverse Mean for Training?" PwC Emerging Technology, September 15. pwc.com/us/en/tech-effect/emerging-tech/virtual-reality-study.html.

Motive.io. n.d. "Mining Safety: South Dakota School of Mines and MSHA." motive.io/customer-stories/mining-safety.

PwC. n.d. "Solving for Skills Training With Virtual Reality." pwc.com/m1/en/services/consulting/technology/emerging-technology/solving-for-skills-training-with-virtual-reality.html.

Tavolieri, J. 2019. "AR & VR Coming To a 'Store' Near You." DiversityMBA Media, December 20. diversitymbamagazine.com/career-development/ar-vr-coming-to-a-store-near-you.

The Ken Blanchard Companies. 2022. "The Ken Blanchard Companies Partners With Immersive Learning Leader Talespin on New Trust VR Simulation." February 15. kenblanchard.com/About-Us/News/Press-Releases/New-Talespin-Trust-VR-Sim.

Van Brenk, D. 2022. "New Virtual-Reality Training Program Gets $1M EPIC Boost." Western News, May 12. news.westernu.ca/2022/05/vr-program-1m-epic-psw.

Virtual Reality Readiness Evaluation Worksheet

When thinking about investing in immersive technology, consider each of the following areas. Talk through them with the leadership and development teams before starting a virtual reality project. Document the responses.

Use Cases
Why do we want to use VR? What are the problems the organization faces?

_____

In which ways could we use virtual reality for training purposes?

_____

Cost
How large or small will the experience be?

_____

What are the associated projected costs, and are they one-time or ongoing?

- Design and development: _____

- Asset and environment creation: _____

- Software: _____

- Hardware: _____

- Mobile device management: _____

- Deployment and delivery: _____

Access
How will learners access the content?

_____

Will we have a bring-your-own-device policy?

_____

Will we purchase devices for each learner or purchase multiple devices that learners can check out to use?

_____

Virtual Reality Readiness Evaluation Worksheet (Cont.)

Can the organization support on-premise Wi-Fi use from required devices?

Can employees have devices shipped to them?

What safety considerations do we need to factor into the learning process?

Data Tracking

How will we track learners and their progress?

What are the necessary steps we need to take to track progress via a learning management system?

How will we capture Experience API data that a traditional LMS doesn't cover?

Do we need to work with an external partner on those matters?

Virtual Reality Project Kickoff Template

Fill in the following information about your virtual reality project.

Use case (Include details about the business problem, business manager, and the reasons VR is the right technology to use):

_____

_____

_____

Learning modalities:

_____

_____

_____

VR team:

- Project manager: _____

- Instructional designer: _____

- Content creator: _____

- Visual designer: _____

- UI/UX designer: _____

- 3D modeler: _____

- Developer: _____

Virtual Reality Project Kickoff Template (Cont.)

Technical skills (Indicate whether internal staff have them or whether you'll need to work with a vendor):

_____

_____

_____

Software:

_____

_____

_____

Hardware:

_____

_____

_____

Potential barriers (These could include costs, organizational culture, leadership doubts, or return on investment):

_____

_____

_____

ATD Press grants permission for the material on this page to be reproduced for personal use.

Bring Training to Life With Virtual Reality | **15**

Upgrade Your **Facilitation Skills** for **Any Modality**

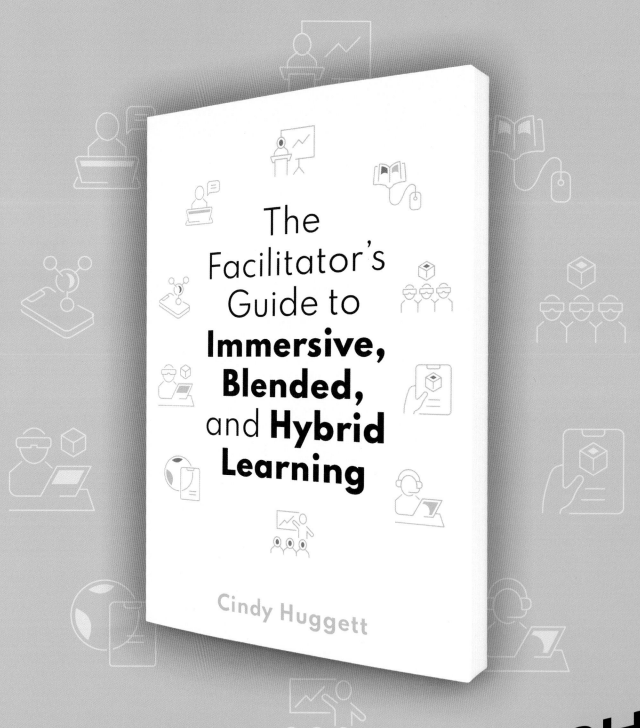

The Facilitator's Guide to **Immersive, Blended,** and **Hybrid Learning**

Cindy Huggett

PRESS